Pearls of Wisdom

Love, Loss, and Liberty

Liz,
Thank-you for always believing in me. I love you so much!

Misty

Pearls of Wisdom

Love, Loss, and Liberty

By: Misty Ely

Bella Esperanza Publishing, LLC

ISBN: 978-0-578-23392-5 (Paperback Edition)
ISBN: 978-1-64921-663-2 (ebook Edition)

Library of Congress Control Number: 2020908646

Cataloging in Publication Data
Author: Misty Pearl Ely
Title: Pearls of Wisdom: Love, Loss and Liberty
Description: Using poetry as a means to discover, reconnect, and heal the human experience while also making it your own.

Editing by Kim Layne, LAc
Printed and bound in the United States of America
First printing June 2020

Bella Esperanza Publishing
A Limited Liability Company
P.O. Box 121007
Arlington, TX 76012

Dedication

This is book is dedicated to all my family and friends who have loved the beautiful and broken parts of me.

To my grandmother for always being my person, my light, and happiness in the world.

Felicity and Julian, may this book serve as a catalyst to spark the flame inside your own soul to pursue your dreams at all costs.

To my fellow Veterans; I love you.

And finally, to the men and women who dedicate their lives to helping each Veteran *come home*; you are noticed, valued, and appreciated.

Epigraph

It is not the critic who counts; not the man who points out how the strong man stumbles, or where the doer of deeds could have done them better. The credit belongs to the man who is actually in the arena, whose face is marred by dust and sweat and blood; who strives valiantly; who errs, who comes short again and again, because there is no effort without error and shortcoming; but who does actually strive to do the deeds; who knows great enthusiasms, the great devotions; who spends himself in a worthy cause; who at the best knows in the end the triumph of high achievement, and who at the worst, if he fails, at least fails while daring greatly, so that his place shall never be with those cold and timid souls who neither know victory nor defeat.

-Theodore Roosevelt

Table of Contents

Preface

Writing has been a part of my life for as long as I can remember. My father often tells a story of me not being allowed to attend kindergarten with my friends because I could read and write so well, instead I got to go straight to first grade. As a child, reading was my escape. I was able to explore far off kingdoms, quench raging fires, tame earthquakes, ride on flying mythical creatures, and dream of tomorrows.

This love for reading and quest for knowledge has continued my whole life and can been seen in my numerous degrees and hundreds (maybe thousands) of books around my house. I often tell my children that I love them more than air, more than water, but not more than books! It is our wonderful silly inside joke and they know I would not be here if not for them.

The Marines taught me about brotherhood, sacrifice, and courage. They gave me a family and they slowly filled a void within myself always searching for adventure and a new beginnings. In Chapter Four you will read poems about my military service and those of my friends. I served nine years on active duty and I am not a combat veteran. However, I was married to a multiple-combat-deployment Marine for over 15 years and we raised our children in that demanding military lifestyle. I am also a therapist to those wounded in war, suffering with the invisible and undeniable scars. Their stories inspired me to write, connect, and share with fellow Veterans as a way to help us all heal.

Like many others, I have experienced more trauma than ever should have been possible. Writing is how I survived. Writing gave me an avenue to process my speechless words, to mend a broken heart, and heal from the inside out. Throughout this book you will undoubtedly feel the pain in my voice and the love in my heart. You will see my pride from being a Marine Corps Veteran and hear stories of not only triumph, but horror as well. Some of the poems are violent, raw, and deeply sad. My intent is to never cause someone harm from reading my words, but instead to shine a light on the fact that we can all overcome the depths of hell-I've been there, let me show you the way out.

Never forget that you are loved, valued, and appreciated for being exactly who you are. In the words of the amazing Hemingway "We are all broken, that's how the light gets in."

ME

hapter One

Life- in all its majestic beauty
and pain.

Do what you can, with what you have,
where you are.

-Theodore Roosevelt

Compass

I've lost my way a time or two
At a crossroad, not knowing what to do
Off the beaten path, I've taken the long way
Every misdirection, brought me to this day
I've been so lost that I couldn't find north
This ever winding journey, bringing me back & forth
The unanswered prayers, misguided course
Like evil always beckoned without remorse
My magnetic north was thrown off balance
Yet I stayed the course without malice
I knew eventually I'd find my place
In due time & at my pace
When I was ready she'd come to me
My compass to guide & set me free
Finally free for the last leg of travel
To put on my armor & face this battle
With you at my side, true north at my back
The time is now for my final attack
Lead the way, for I will follow
And where we walk, it shall be hallowed

Ready, Set

She's unbelievably vulnerable
And immeasurably scared
She's patiently waited,
For the crisis she's prepared
She tries not to crumble
With the boulders upon her back
No longer afraid, braced for the attack
She won't be caught unaware,
This much you can bet
Throughout the years she's learned
This game of roulette
She once was timid
And would cower beneath your hand
She'll get hit again,
Only when you learn to count sand
She still walks with this shadow,
Still flinches to some degree
But you'd be wise not to mistake
This gesture for sympathy

Mountains

I'm standing at the base and wondering why I want to climb
Another mountain to conquer, maybe another place in time
With each step I take, I remember another place I've been
The battles I've lost and all the sin
I remember each face, because they are burned in my soul
The piercing cries of agony, the misfortunes untold
My face burns in the sun, my feet blister in their shoes
But I climb ever more, because I'm not facing the truth
I'm trying so hard to live, but I'm barely getting by
I try to focus on the good, but the mountains stack high
They're vast & wide, & too many to count
The conquest doesn't matter, because they surmount
I walk, I run, I climb & crawl
Always waiting to break my fall
Each step I take brings me closer to the end
It's not the summit I want, it's the ascent
But these mountains are mine & mine alone
Each beautifully complicated, majestically shown
I climb them with pride & my dignity intact
I might not always have the strength, but I'm coming back
And they'll be there, waiting for when I can
Because these are my mountains, they're in my hands.

Raconteuse

A true raconteuse, she weaves the plot
Seeking only closure, for what she's got
To end the pain, to see the light
Using all her strength to stand the fight
This last story, it's hers alone
Finally realizing what she's always known
She flips the page, it's blank & clear
Time to write the story without the fear
This new chapter is bold & brave
Wrapped in confidence, not well-behaved
Inside her the light burns bright
Putting an end to those sleepless nights
She's ready now, pen in hand
To write her script like no one can

Anchor

I was this ship, long ago lost at sea
Left to wander the ocean, not a soul missing me
No purpose I had, broken beyond compare
Too many things to be fixed, no burden to share
So I drifted alone, controlled by none
Rebelling the current, a journey for one
Along the way, someone took notice
Started making repairs & made promise
They promised to guide me, to lead the way
To bury the past, to find promise each day
They gave me an anchor to deploy when lost
With the reassurance that love does not cost
I don't have to be alone; I can choose to be free
With my anchor attached, I believe in me
I can steer my own course, drift no more
I'm ready to dock at the harbor & walk about the shore

Beach

She sat on the beach and watched the waves roll in
The tears on her cheeks told of the pain within
She glared at the moon, fascinated by its light
The encompassing hope is what she needed tonight
She studied the stars and how delightful they were
Like millions of diamonds, their beauty pure
She sat up and ran her toes through the sand
But she needed something, something in her hand
She reached into the dark for a person that wasn't there
Just to be reminded of the reason why she sits here
She is scared, alone and sad
Her family miles away, no friends she had
She looks out into the open and sees it stretch forever
Is this how long her torment will last, is the end a never
She stands and turns to face the ocean
Jump in, turn around, it's all emotion
As she walks back to her car, she sees a ray of light
Maybe God was listening, He heard her prayers tonight

Gray

I love the gray
it soothes my soul
Blankets the horizon
pays the toll
Without the gray
I have to see
The vastness of colors
surrounding me
In its embrace
the truth is vague
Allowing honesty
to be the plague
Why can't I wander
lost in the abyss
Never finding love
will it I miss
If I can't be true
can't be open
I lose the words
never spoken

Lessons

What have you learned in divorce?
That sometimes love requires a different course
What have you learned by being a parent?
That there's no greater gift on this planet
What have you learned about being in love?
That when two souls connect, it's fireworks from above
What have you learned about being a wife?
That it takes two to choose a course in life
What have you learned about being a daughter?
That emulating your parents is not worth the bother
What have you learned by being a friend?
That the purest of love comes from within
What have you learned about being a mom?
That those two heart beats are my little song
What have you learned about who you are?
That life is a journey and I'm here to go far

Perspective

Eleven little letters make up this word
But the dichotomy it creates is all but absurd
Are we all too evolved to see the others view
With our rose-colored glasses thinking our past is new
Not understanding all the things we can lose
Blind with ambition, it is the path we choose
History teaches us again and again
That we'll pay for these burdens, have time to mend
But what if we paused, took notice, and adjusted
And sought first to understand, perspective is trusted

Maybe

Maybe when I'm older, I'll take time to smell the roses
Maybe when I'm older, I'll had made better choices
Maybe when I'm older, I'll have a house and a family too
Maybe when I'm older, I will have someone like you
Maybe when I'm older, I'll understand why
Maybe when I'm older, I won't be afraid to die
Maybe when I'm older, all the answers will be in my grasp
Maybe when I'm older, I won't always just fall short of last
Maybe when I'm older, I'll learn to love and give love in return
And maybe when I'm older, I'll be happy because it is my turn

Phoenix

I see her fly, among the clouds
In the setting sun, or snowy downs
She's magnificent, with wings of gold
Shimmering purples, captivating and bold
With sapphire eyes, as deep as the ocean
Her gaze can cause quite the commotion
She's the symbol of hope, even in death
From fiery ashes, she does step
Her rebirth awakens my spirit
With her, I found my merit
This icon of a new beginning
My phoenix, life unending

Yearning

She stands a little taller now
Some respect she has earned
It came with a heavy price
These lessons she learned
She hasn't yet reached her potential
And she's still scared of the unknown
But somehow she's found the courage
To face whatever's thrown
She still longs for acceptance
Constantly needing positive praise
Wanting to belong
Yet lost within this maze
For everything she is
And everything she will become
She still lies alone in bed
With fears of what's to come

Waves

Whoa, steady, steady I say
I take the helm and lead us today
Not knowing where I'm going
But the vast open is better than knowing
I know where I've been
I know what I've seen
I know what I've done
This path made for me
I'm in this storm, where I'm holding on tight
Waves crack against my bow, I tremble in fright
I'm built strong, I'm built tough
But has this life taught me enough
To withstand the pain, for a brighter tomorrow
A burial at sea, for no more sorrow
An avalanche of loss, a flood so vast
That an outcry of love is all that lasts
These are my waves that beckon now
Named courage & hope, and begin with how
They are quite beautiful, stunning in the sun
And I have a feeling, this voyage has just begun

Warmth

Warmth, like the soft glow of the fireplace
As it blankets the room and we feel safe
Warmth, like the embrace of your children
Strong and steady as all you believe in
Warmth, like a home cooked meal with company
you love
Simple reminders of your blessings and God's grace
above.

Believable Lies

I'm stronger than I think
Ready to bounce within a blink
I think I've found the missing link

Everyday there's a struggle in my mind
Pondering the reflection, trying to be kind
Within my heart, no words to find

The constant chaos that always ensues
Binding my eyes to find the clues
Stumbling & falling within the news

Grasping at straws, holding my breath
Another day's met with another regress
Too much on my plate, though I digress
This life of mine, what a mess

How true is that statement, rooted in lies
Healing alone in this disguise
Yearning for love, I'll meet my demise

So what's this link, that is the key
Like the smoldering sun, it's blinding me
Yet I stand on this doorstep ready to see

Get out of your way
Is all I can say
Silence your mind and live for today

Chapter Two

Darkness- the end that always comes, allowing ourselves to mourn, grieve, scream in anger, and release the pain within.

He who has a why to live for can bear with almost any how.

-Nietzsche
also quoted by
Victor Frankl

Darkness Falls

Darkness falls we run and hide
Screams echo far and wide
The piercing cries that haunt our soul
Riveting flashbacks take their toll
Delusions of peace give us reprieve
One moment of clarity is all we conceive
We welcome the sandman and the reaper too
Bringing with them hallucinations of you
Of course I see you when I sleep
The only chance I get to have a peek
I close my eyes to bring you here
Just have to fight the blood curdling fear
You're gone and I know
This pain, I still show
It beckons me near from my core
To squander my hope forever more
The darkness falls, I won't run and hide
Listen to my screams as we stand side by side
Together we can tackle this nightmare of mine
Because you're haunted too, by father time

See Me

See me
I'm right here
Not trying to hide
Welcoming disgrace, we sit side by side
See me
Open your eyes
Take it all in
I'm sick of the fighting, I'm not your friend
See me
I wanted to be your partner for life
But I failed repeatedly and caused this strife
See me
Standing here
Losing it all
Wanting to be more than just someone you call
See me
I asked for too much
And you gave too little
Stuck in purgatory neither wanting to settle
See me
Lost and confused
Broken and bruised
Empty and scared, neither one prepared
See me
See me now as I walk away
See me now as I say
That it's too late for us this day
See me
See me now, see me at last
As I put this marriage in the past
See me at last stand tall and fight
See what's always been in your sight

What If

What if I hadn't known hell
And I had no story to tell
What if the beatings had never come
And I never felt the proper shun
What if this pain was not given a price
'Cause the price I paid was not too nice
What if my journey had begun with love
Instead I was raised with an iron glove
What if that night I had pulled the trigger
No more suffering to remember
What if he'd listened when I said no
When I told him to stop and let me go
What if the day you held that shot gun tight
I wouldn't have begged for you to spare his life
What if every violent act I endured
Enabled me to do some good
What if I could take this trauma that I know
And use it to help people begin to grow
What if I gave a voice to all that pain
I'd learn the suffering wasn't in vain
What if through my healing process
I embraced my own acceptance
What if I realized that the memories are there
As part of my being, but no longer fear
What if finally, I understand
That you can't take my hope, no one can
What if I now know the choice is mine
Because all I got left is plenty of time

Better Man

Why can't you see the growth I've made
A certain quiet beyond the shade
You control the game with highest spade
Shattering my soul like a hand grenade

I beg for you to love me again
You smile in my face and try to pretend
I search your eyes for a chance you send
But you don't even treat me as a friend

I know I've done wrong, an illustrious past
I've apologized for years, but your anger lasts
You want out of this life, your net is cast
As you start to run, my pace is fast

And here is the problem, let's give it a name
How about trauma, depression and shame
How about constant failure and placing the blame
Having the losing hand in every game

I keep trying to prove I'm a better man
But now I see, you are no fan
Because in this chaos you learned you can
Survive on your own without this man

Which is fine and I really do understand
But why can't you tell me this is the end
I'm ready to listen, so let's begin
Because I'm beyond ready for my heart to mend

Depression

Depression consumes me; it overwhelms me in every
way
My mind races, anxiety constantly over takes me
How do I quiet the storm
How do I calm the beast
How do I let down this wall
To allow my monsters to creep
I balance between anger and love, joy and pain
Yet everyone I need, I push away
Could they really handle seeing my pain
Yet when I don't allow them in, I still pass the blame
Am I always right or always wrong
This fine line of just getting along
Is the answer in that glass or in this bottle
In those pills or do we settle
How do you begin to feel right
When everything is still so wrong
How do you keep going
When you are no longer strong
The failures mount high
Disappointment is the norm
How to choose not to die and weather the storm
This would mean you still have hope
I guess that's all you need in order to cope

Dark As Death

Dark as death, Cold as snow,
My body is dead, so let me go.

I've passed away,
This is best,
So go on with your life,
With all the rest.

The past has gone.
The future has to come,
It's not your fault for what I've done.

I'm sorry it happened.
I had to do this,
Just go on,
I know I will be missed.

Dark as death, Cold as snow,
My body is dead, so let me go.

You knew I was going to go,
But you didn't know when,
I'm sorry it came now,
Instead of then.

You say there is a reason,
But not one to be shown,
Just give it up,
And leave it alone.

You can't change what's already done,
Don't even try,
Just stop and say goodbye.

Dark as death, Cold as snow,
My body is dead, so let me go.

Meat

Primed and ready for the beast
After all, I am the feast
Your gaze uneasy, the stare too long
No need to fight, I will belong
How come I surrender every time
Is the fate no longer mine
Why say no-you will not hear
I know what's next, no need to fear
Where is my voice
Where is my choice
Far too many things to rejoice
So that's it then
You will win
Because the battle is not worth the fight
I've lost my pawn, but not my knight

Not Ready

Into the gates of hell I plunge so deep
Shut them off or let them creep
Locked away, yet still they seep
No longer these secrets can I keep

Bury the one or bury them all
Refuse they exist and take the fall
Why the hell share, it's your call
Give them a voice & I become small

I have to admit that I've done wrong
In no part of me is that my song
I can carry this load; I'm that strong
Actually, I've done it for very long

So keep your words, I'll be on my way
You have nothing to offer is what I say
I'm not ready to change, not this day
Let me live my life in dismay

Now

You miss me now -
Not when I was there
When I loved you immensely -
And you didn't care
You want me now -
My entire body to enjoy
Not like when you had me -
Oh so very coy
You need me now -
Daily struggles are too much
Never once did you appreciate -
All the things you didn't touch
You love me now -
Because you've lost me for sure
Time to paste on a smile -
And hope for a cure
But now, now you hate me -
Because you finally see
That I've found peace -
And oh, the possibility

Surrender

Crying & crying this pain never ends
A life devoid of love is on the mend
How do I cope in search of a fix
I'll pop these pills & the drink I mix
Because that's the answer, self-medicate it is
Why the hell be present in this life to live
I feel like I'm spiraling, a tornado over water
A hurricane over land
It's all confused, yet here I stand
Tormented and twisted, invisible and raw
Stumbling forward on my hands I crawl
A kick in the face, a knee to the chest
I steady my footing, prepare for the rest
You beat me down, yet I rise again
Three steps forward and back you send
I'm bloodied and broken, this reflection I don't know
Where the hell is my strength, my courage to grow
I try to walk, but I can't even stand
You've taken it all so where do I land
I guess I don't know, you've won this fight
I'll wave my flag, I'm done for tonight

The Rape

I still remember
I remember it all
The pain, the hurt, the loss of my innocence
I remember the betrayal, the rumors, the gossip
The images of you over me
Holding your hand over my mouth
Pushing me to the bed
I remember the ripping pain of my virginity and
The tears I tried to hide
I remember you telling me to shut-up so no one would hear
What you were doing to me in the room next to where my
brothers slept
I remember you climbed in my window those few nights
While I laid frozen with fear and shame
I remember how you made friends with my family
Because they never knew the true monster of you
All these things I remember so vividly and I will never for-
get
I chose to not let them consume my days and nights any
longer
You tormented my nights for years
You have ruined every romantic, sexual, and intimate rela-
tionship I have ever had
You caused me more pain than I could ever express in
words
I will never forgive you, but I am learning to forgive myself
I am learning how to love, trust and be whole again
I deserve to be happy, loved and valued
This has been a long horrible journey
And I am who I am today because of the choices I have
made
The hardest thing to learn was accepting that it was not my
fault.

No More To Give

Crying alone
Drinking alone
Hurting alone
Die alone
Live alone
Be alone
Always alone

Why this
Why now
Why me
Why care
Why learn   I just can't
Why need   I just won't
Why breathe   I just don't
                    I just should
Hope gone   I just could
Love gone   I just would
Truth gone   I just know
Desire gone
Lust gone
Happy gone
Be gone

Know nothing
Know more
Know less
Know fake
Know kind
Know bitterness
Know forever more this
is a test
- I chose not to play

Spiraling

Spinning I spiral
Like dust in the wind
Within the grips of gravity
Heavy laden by sin

Bouncing and blundering
What a mess I've made
Trying to find myself
While lurking in shade

Luminous and lost
And lazy at times
Each calculated step
Another landmine

To safely sabotage
My ridiculous dreams
Mourn their loss
With silent screams

A vibrant visionary
I thought I was
A ticking time bomb
And the j**udge**

Quiz and question
Why my sleep departs
Insomnia beckons me
                For this I'll start

This chaos and crazy
Can't be all that's left
Give me a glimmer
Something magnificent

Shoulder my fears
Get out of my head
Insanity leers

Pull me in
As I pull away
If the doubt creeps in
I will decay

Pathways

The path I chose to take
The life I often fake
The choices that I make
Decide the future I cannot shake
To leave others in my wake
Feel the pressure of the break
The sorrow, my tears but a lake
Constantly waiting for that quake
I pretend and eat the cake
In the garden, I am the snake
Poise to strike, for this my sake
On the defensive, I overtake
Lost and alone in this mistake
Try with my might to remake
This is mine to forsake

Lonely

Lonely that is how I feel
Scared because it is all too real
Anger that seems to be my answer
So many problems spreading like cancer
Happiness comes at such a cost
I think we are all a little lost
Torment and pain haunt my night
Hopeful prospects invade my light
Empty and raw I am again
Why do I always let you in
Mindful of the time and the journey to come
Even bending & flexing, molding as one
So why the loneliness, I only seek to be heard
This concept of reality a bit too absurd
Memories & magic & childhood dreams
Make a person believe it could be more than it seems

Overdrawn

Woe is me
This I see
My reality
What to be
Who are we
Pawns in uniformity
Marching blissfully
Nowhere to flee
On bended knee
We take the key
Doors open nobly
Where's the family
Gone to misery
Alone in this soliloquy
I am the fee
My debt to insanity

Suppose To Be

You were suppose to be my anchor
My light on the shore
Guiding me for safe passage
With promises of forever more

You were suppose to be my king
Not to rule over me
But let me be your queen

You were suppose to believe in us
When all hope was gone
When I'm truly broken
Not sure if I'll see dawn

You were suppose to be my true love
My very last first kiss
How did I have it all wrong
And yet your love I miss

Angel Rene

My sweet little Angel, how I dread this time of year
As I look back on my life and the birthdays we'll never share
I often dream of what you would be become
A scholar or chef, my first-born son
I remember the day, when they told me you died
I was scared and alone, in that hospital I cried
Then came the waiting and the surgery that almost cost both our lives
Constantly hemorrhaging under their knives
Then I woke up broken body and broken heart
Wishing I'd died too instead of living apart
The next few weeks passed in a blur
Blood work, more tests, medication I'm sure
Everyone's well wishes and encouragement to move on
But I was hollow inside, barely getting along
Your daddy picked me up from that nursery floor more times that I can count
Even when I climbed inside your crib, he pulled me out
He was my strength in those dismal October days
He reminded me how to live is more that I can say
14 years have passed and I still grieve your loss
But I'll always be your mother, and I'll carry this cross

I Weep

I weep for all the things I do not know and for all
the things I do
I weep because you're in pain and there's nothing
I can do
I weep next to you as you struggle to find comfort
with the new scars from today
I weep as I listen to the rhythm in your breath as
slumber finds its way
I weep knowing that our time together will one
day end
I weep because I am not sure how I will ever
mend
I weep inside and slowly mourn the loss of the
greatest person I ever knew
I weep and I pray with every fiber that you know I
love you

Suicide Note

The act of taking one's life voluntarily
When all the pieces align before you clearly
When taking one last breath seems the right choice
Weighing out the options and you have no remorse
I'm ready to end it all and it's about time
So sick of the pain and hurt paradigm
I'm tired of people saying it will get better
You don't live in my shoes, you're no pace setter
I drown my feelings in alcohol
Look at the phone and wish you would call
But then I hate myself because your voice I don't want
to hear
You've tormented my life for so many years
I want to die, so when you bury me you will know
That you caused this pain in me to show
That it was more than I could bear
That I would rather die than live another day here
Because what's the point as I cry tonight
You've taken it all no end in sight
I want to die, that's all I want
But in living, you still get to taunt
What if you had to bury me
To live with the memory you had to see
As they lowered me in the ground
Those M16 shots heard all around
For you to know that you caused this pain
That you slowly drove me insane

Enter Psyche

Why are we so scared of the truth?
Because we fear what we don't know, or do we really
fear the truth?
Is it better to live in fear, than face your own reality?
For most of us, our perceptions are reality.
Therefore if we change what we perceive, will the fear
disappear?
Will the truth be known, if we own our power and
choose a brighter, honest path?
Will our destiny be illuminated, with the journey we
should take?
Why, then are we so scared of the truth?

Puppet

Play me once, play it fast
Either way, You're still in last
But do you even care
Better to live in constant fear
It doesn't matter if you have a plan
You're in my life as a man
Which means you serve but one need
To take my body & plant your seed
I have no more to give, no love to share
So, take what you want, I don't care
It's what I'm used to, what I was born to fulfill
My happiness was never part of the deal
According to your God, I'm here to serve my
man
Until I wither and die and turn to sand
And from those ashes, shall I be born free
Absolutely not, because hell delivered me
So, I'll say it again, because I'm sure you don't
understand
Play with me all you want, then put the puppet

Black Or White

I can't be black or white
I don't even want to try
I want to live in the shadows
Give no voice to the cry
It's not that easy
Or it's not for me
Because one of us will lose
In this game, you see
If I let you in
Bring down the wall
Allowing you a glance
What if I fall
What if I can't run
What if I stay
What if I love you
Believe the words you say
And you break me
Could I heal once more
Black or white
Gray at the core

Be Damned

I'm not you and you're not me
I'm sick and tired of trying to make you see
What's in my heart, we're a world apart
Why even start, you're in the dark
And missed the mark

But you know it all,
As I fall
Making me feel so very small
Pinned against this concrete wall
The shadowed reflection of a doll

Who am I now
Who was I then
Where lies the truth
When all I do is pretend

I will be your perfect
I will be your muse
Because finding myself
Is making me confused

You're only here to speak
Listening for the weak
The timid and the meek
Often slaughtered like the sheep
So much for the company we keep

This isn't the version of me
That I want others to see
I need control in some degree
Please don't give me your sympathy

Walk a mile in my shoes
I'm not an open book
Cut me some slack for once
Give the pain in my eyes a look

I don't think you can
Even if your tried
Because you broke the law tonight
When you told me that I lied

There's names you can say
There's hurt thrown my way
But not a single day
Shall my integrity sway

What you've shown me tonight
Is to hold my cards tight
No vulnerability in sight
Once again you've broken my might

hapter Three

Love– and the complicated, messy, glorious parts about it that make us yearn for more.

You know you're in love when you can't fall asleep because reality is finally better than your dreams.

-Dr. Seuss

Love Story

It's like an enchanted world, we've entered in
It's like a symphony of music with no end
It's like your very first kiss and how exciting it was
It's like not wanting more, but nothing less just be-
cause
It's like an overwhelming joyous occasion
It's like wanting and needing without hesitation
It's like super natural powers to use as you please
It's like a monopoly of feelings that does not cease
It's like the assurance that your love will stand the
test of time
It's like knowing without a doubt that you will al-
ways be mine

The Man Of My Dreams

He'll be my lover and my best friend
He'll be all I ever wanted in a man
He'll open doors and pull out chairs
Be Mr. Prince Charming and always be there
He'll listen to my worries, give me guidance in the
end
Make me laugh out loud and always hold my hand
He'll kiss me in public, wrap his arm around my waist
Hold me close to him, while people notice his great
taste
He'll always be a gentleman and put me before him
Do anything to make me happy, so he can see my big
grin
He'll comment on my smile and how nice I look
Be always willing to help out and maybe even cook
He'll want to go to church and pray with me too
Take the kids to school, have brunch at noon
My dreams and ambitions are as important to him as
me
He'll give me inspiration in everything I see
He'll come into my life when I need him most
And he'll never let me go, because we are this close

Horizon

This place is serene
More beauty than I've ever seen
A simple reflection glistening
By all accounts, inspiring
The water rises, ebbs & flows
The waves crest, there it goes
With every peak, it starts to slow
Creating the need, for it to grow
Upon the sand, they meet at last
Where wet and dry are now the past
My footprints linger, the dye is cast
Another wave begins all too fast
Does this turquoise water ever end
Where does that magnificent sky yet begin
This uncomplicated beauty it does lend
To the profound understanding of our horizon

Starting

I'm starting to blossom
I'm starting to bloom
I'm going to glow
As I enter the room

I'm starting to see
My true self
And I'm going to love her
Like no one else

I'm starting to forgive
And learning to move on
There's a rhythm in my step
And I've found a new song

I'm starting to believe
In my dreams once more
Finding my confidence
And sounding more sure

I'm starting to think
I may be worth the chance
Maybe smile again
And go for a dance

I'm starting to accept
I've found so much hope
I'm writing endless words
Within them I cope

I'm starting to imagine
All the things to come
Rediscovering who I am
And just how much I've done

I'm starting to trust
And follow this heart of mine
Because I finally know
That it's my time

Art Reciprocated

If I called him an artist
What would you think
Would you believe in his greatness
This century's missing link
With a pencil in hand
A masterpiece he will create
Letting the picture transform
In your heart to resonate
A novelist and poet
His words dance across the page
Leaving you yearning for more
A mere spectator to his stage
His voice beckons
For you to hear
A thunderous tone
Yet soothes the fear
He is a maestro
A true creator of art
With a vault of knowledge
Making him indescribably smart
He does not believe in favorites
He enjoys it all
From classic literature to music
Nothing is too small
There's a buoyancy in his step
When he creates at will
Because true creative genius
Is an unbridled skill
Journals of thoughts
Scattered throughout his room
His walls a canvas
So stay tuned
He will create, he will live
And he will thrive
He's found the artist in his soul
Now he's truly alive

Love

I love hard and strong
I love with all my might
I love too much some times
I love good and bad
I love without prejudice
I love until it hurts
I love that I can't stop
I love to love
I love honestly and purely
I love even when it's impossible
I love against the odds
I love for those who can't
And most importantly-I love because I can

Rain

The pitter pat of rain drops fall
All around me I feel the calm
The soothing sound I love to hear
Brings me peace and out of fear
I stare at it, wondering if it knows
Just how much I love to see it grow
Bring on the thunder, lightning too
It feeds my soul, as do you
I want to walk in the rain
Hold your hand so tight
Feel the wetness of each drop
And the raw beauty in sight
The cleansing it conveys
The promise of a new day
A simple understanding, yet vaguely known
A gift from above, that's rarely shown
My slumber comes, with you in my ear
Whispering pitter pat, fall asleep my dear

My Proposal

There's this walk I'd like to take
My hand in yours beside the lake
Fall leaves color all around
Simple bliss without a sound
Flying fish jump here and there
The water glistens in the morning air
This is perfect, I can't look away
In your embrace is where I'll stay
We reach a clearing beyond the path
You've orchestrated this perfect math
From your satchel you remove a quilt
I lay it out, as you knelt
From your pocket you retrieve a ring
I swear to God, heaven sings
You take my hand & profess your love
In your eyes I see above
I see the promises and adventures
Life's little tests and tantrums
I see it all clear as day
On this beautiful morning in May
I put my hands upon your face
And say yes at cyclic pace
Lightning fast I'm in your arms
You pick me up with no alarm
You twirl me about and kiss my lips
Tears flowing rapidly in all of this
You promise to love me like no one can
You're the embodiment of my perfect man
We are so happy and our future is bright
I've been waiting an eternity for my white knight

I Hate You

So there's this mirror and I hate it
Actually, I hate all mirrors
Because I hate me
I hate my face
I hate my thighs
I hate my butt and my eyes
I hate my stomach and the stretch marks
I hate my shortness and all these birthmarks
I hate every mole and scar I have
I hate my feet and my skinny calves
I hate my voice and my gray hair
I hate my acne and my skin that is too fair
I hate everything from my fingers to my toes
But most of all I hate me because I know
I know why I feel this way and why I should not
I know why my mind will not allow me to love myself
I know that I am smart, brilliant in fact
But this does not change my reality
I am the product of years of torment
I hear those voices declaring worthlessness, ugly,
dumb, and useless
No amount of accomplishments has been able to
stop the voices
Why
How can I ever really love another, when I hate my-
self with every fiber of my being?

I Love You

So there's this girl and I love her
I love her more than I ever thought I could
Because she's me
I love my heart shaped face
I love my runner-girl thighs
I love my perfect butt and ever changing eyes
I love my stomach and my stretch marks because
they remind me of the babies I've carried
I love my height and all these birthmarks because it
shows I'm varied
I love every mole and scar I have, what a beautiful
canvas God has created
I love my fair skin, simply amazing and understated
I love myself from my fingers to my toes
But most of all I love me because I know
I know what it's like to feel love and to be in love
I know I have the choice and the right to both
I am brilliant and kind
I am a giver and lover
There's no better combination to find in another
I am worthy and I'm worth it
I'm a best friend, a mother and a social worker
They are not my jobs, they are who I am
And I'm totally in love with me.

Ms. ME

My mind is frantic, so many things to do
But who made these lists, other than you
You drive yourself mad, trying to do everything right
Why is being miss perfect always such a fight
Do you crave the constant turmoil, love all the stress
Or do you stay busy to hide your life's mess
If you slow down, do you hate what you see
Or does it remind you of where you should be
Could be, should be, and what ifs
What is a hit and what is a miss
Can you handle being alone with your thoughts
Are you driven by the have and have not's
How about trying to live your life looking through the
windshield
Vice the rearview mirror
Life might look a tad bit clearer
Be present in the moment, be here
Take time to enjoy life and care
Bask in the joys, talk about the pain
But most importantly
Try to live life to the fullest each day

Wanted Ad

I want an avid reader
And a poet too
A magical story teller
Romancing the truth
I want wisdom
And knowledge overflowing my glass
Someone to challenge my thoughts
Without the clash
To be fully attuned
To what I must say
To lose himself in me
Each day
Spending hours and hours
Soaking it all in
Until our brains hurt
And we feel grand
We drink in the words
Digest it all
Literary genius
In us does fall
He writes
And I listen
I write
And he hears
Our simple writings
Have torn down our fears
Because true poetry is art
And there's no better way
To explain your emotions
And what you're trying to say
This gift is unique, bestowed upon a few
Can everything I want, really be found within you

Inamorata

True love-no two words in the English language, have
been more searched
It's a spellbinding mystery, its own research
Looking for the impossible, when the data is clear
Is it better to settle, then to live alone in fear
Wouldn't you fight and risk it all
For that chance at love, no matter the fall
To be the sparkle in someone's eye
To be the beginning and the end, with no goodbye
To live fully and completely, like never before
And to truly understand, there can be more
There can be love, without pain
There can be love, without shame
There can be love, that's pure and honest
There can be love, that's not a contest
This is our kind of love, in its rawest form
Extraordinarily perfect and taken us by storm
To believe of a magic, that we've only read in books
A mythical ending that surely, we mustn't look
But as fate would have it, the stars aligned
And it's not long enough, this life time
My happy ending and yours too
It's really just the beginning of me and you

Be Yourself

It's funny a thing how fate works
Imagine the possibilities never falling too short
To answer one's dreams in the blink of an eye
Seeing the reality of your fantasies and being mine
Opening up to a world of new things to share
Exploring each other, without a care
Not being ashamed of who you really are
Letting the other one see, this is you by far
And as they lead into this vast uncertainty of this
Hearts and minds are often lost, but rarely ever
missed

Adorn

I adore you, he whispers in my ear
My favorite three words, that extinguish the fear
How I've longed for this, this kind of romance
It catches you off guard, a certain happenstance
The butterflies flutter, I'm nervous and unsure
Searching for his approval, as our eyes meet at the door
One date, turns into two, days into weeks
Enveloped in your arms, your love is all I seek
The comfort of your embrace, beautiful love we make
The joining of our souls, indeed makes the earth quake
You're my everything and everything I seem to need
My complicated giver, helping this advocate to succeed
One look in those eyes and I'm instantly lost
Your reassuring gaze reminds me love doesn't cost
Running your fingers through my hair
So many gestures to show that you care
You're my perfect and I hope I don't have this amiss
Because I am willing and ready to put my all into this

Dreams

What is life without dreams
But to see hope in all things
To allow that picture, we see in our mind
To flourish in sight, all in due time
To dream is to live and to live is to dream
To be vulnerable in the moment is harder than it
seems
We need to believe that we deserve to be whole
That dreams are attainable and not to let go
There are no time limits for your dreams to come true
Believe in your mind, hope with your heart, and follow
through.

Forgiven

I can't stand any longer
I don't have the strength
Locking my legs in fear
Refusing to fall beneath
Letting go of shame
And ideas of perfection
Kneeling before you now
Searching for my reflection
There's no greater love
And there's nothing I want more
Than You at my side
For this I am sure
Yearning for acceptance
And to know I am forgiven
I'll cast away my will
And in Your light, I'll live in

The Hemingway Effect

He uses the English language
To plot a story never managed
He fabricates a version beyond compare
Heart pounding, page turning, enraptured despair
You fight, and yearn, and plead
For the characters to succeed
That their story will be the one
Where dreams come true, mankind has won
But alas, he reminds us that this is not the case
Because happily ever after is a bittersweet taste
Our story begins & ends like the cast
Two lonely people falling too fast
Our first touch electric, smoldering lust
And this was only after we began to trust
Our written words, our spoken vows
The physical touch, always around
Then like the reaper, the powers that be
Made us decide, him or me
So horribly tragic, to stay or to leave
To give up on love, yet still believe
What did he teach us, Hemingway in observation
To never have loved at all is the worst expression
So I'll raise my glass and propose a toast
To adventure ahead and learning to coast
To believing in magic, a book with no end
And that you, young Hemingway, are indeed my best
friend

Sleep

The world is sleeping and I lie awake
No counting sheep for my sake
Is it stress, anxiety or too many to list
The constant feeling there's something I missed
The forever cycle of ups and downs
I'm like a princess that has lost her crown
I want to rest, I need it so
Exhaustion is luminous, but where to go
Soothing sounds, deep breathing and such
They help for a minute, then not so much
My mind is invaded by things to come
So many lists and things to get done
How about you pull me close and hold me tight
Whisper you love me and tell me good night
I think that's the answer to this riddle of time
That I'm tired of sleeping alone in this bed of mine
Maybe all I need is a heartbeat to hear
Protected in your embrace, my mind will clear
This simple gesture, that you will protect all
May be just what I need to make these eye lids fall

I Don't Know

If I could explain the way I feel
My emotions souring, a journey of will
Sometimes when I look in your eyes I see
A glimmer of retreat, can this be
Can I honestly trust you from all ends
To do as you say, as we now begin
So many questions and what ifs
So much hurt and pain, can we handle this
Is the truth really what flows from your lips
Or is it promises that you'll never miss
Are we just to comfort each other in our time of need
Will it last forever, is that long enough indeed
Do you love me as much as I love you
Is this where we fall together or say we are through

My Second Self

How would you define a friend
More than family, heaven sent
More than the words of encouragement
More than just my safety net
Crying on her shoulders
Too many times to count
When I'm hanging by a thread
Demons mount
When I'm in a black hole
My abyss
Trying to figure it all out
There she is
She listens close
And holds me tight
Ever reassuring
It will be alright
But she's more than a friend
A teacher too
I can't put into words
The things I've learned from you
She sends me random pics
Just to make me smile
Support me from afar
When I run those miles
And what absolutely
Means the most
She loves me for me
We're this close

Reset

I'm both scared and excited for the same reason
Is it really my time to shine, is this my season
I'm starting this new chapter and I'm nervous as hell
Because I've never focused on me having a story to tell
I've always done for others, been a mom, wife and friend
But in this moment in time, all I want is my heart to mend
I want to focus on my dreams and all the goals I can reach
I need to save my life and then begin to teach
I want to show the world that we are not our past
That change is hard, but love & loyalty will last
I want to believe that I deserve all things to come
I'll give you everything I have and then some
I'm ready and willing to pay the price
Life's a gamble, let's roll the dice
That's funny because you know that's not me
I need to plan and control, make a list you see
I need to feel I have the power and the right to choose
I'm no one's puppet anymore; I get to be the muse
So here's to new beginnings, laying this fear to rest
I'm pretty sure it's time, for me to try my best

hapter Four

Military– the unspoken, behind the scenes protectors of our freedoms. We number but a few, however our impact cannot be measured in words, quantified by deeds, or replicated by those who have never worn the uniform.

Wars are not paid for in wartime,

the bill comes later.

-Benjamin Franklin

The Marine

From inside my tent, I could barely see the sun rise
I ponder the day's events of both torment and surprise
To catch them off guard was indeed the plan
How to succeed with my life was the problem at hand
I have to be smarter & faster, and two steps ahead
Never to be left alone to end up dead
I have to protect the lives around me
And give up mine freely for their safety
I have to always be willing to go out on a limb
To provide the blanket of freedom in which my family
lives in
I stand up and put my pack on
Look out into the clearing and see life gone
With this simple gesture, I know it's time
To return to the battlefield, to serve on the line
As we step off, I say a little prayer and hope my family
knows
That when the war is over, this Marine will be coming
home

911

An American tragedy is what we behold
Our worst fears answered as the events unfold
From disbelief to anger, frustration, and sorrow
Holding on to hope and praying for tomorrow
As a nation we are weakened, but steady on our feet
Caught off guard by this attack, but far from retreat
We will answer this threat by nothing more
Than a willingness to succeed, by or by not war
We walk shoulder to shoulder, hand and hand
Singing the National Anthem again and again
We show our perseverance, faith, and pride
In every aspect of diversity far and wide
We are Americans; this is our country and our land
Freedom belongs to us, united we stand

Commencement

Today we pause and reflect on your journey
Where you accomplished goals and began a new story
You chose a path traveled by few
Awakening the warrior that lies within you
You stayed the course even when pain beckoned each
day
You learned to cope with love and hate, even through
dismay
Steadfast in your morals with dignity and respect
Endless opportunities before you honorably met
The dawn has risen, the dark days past
You're welcomed home with friends that last
As you end this chapter and start anew
Remember each of us here is fighting for you
You are worthy and loved, and more resilient than you
believe
So, go forth and carry out every dream you can con-
ceive

Letters Back Home

These letters tell a story, never written in just haste
Because they belong to a Veteran, in another time and
place
They convey more than words, emotions placed in ink
Through this scripted passage, we escape in a blink
We can reflect on our loved ones, simple pleasures
from back home
A tangible letter, yet priceless beauty is shown
Carried safely, tucked away with great care
Each letter a reminder, to help replace the fear
Because reality is, we are on the front lines
Where danger is paramount and no one knows their
time
So I'll steal away these moments, pull my letter from its
spot
Remember that I'm loved; your freedom is why I
fought

Veteran

Among them all, a few did stand
Men and women joined hand in hand
They fight for America, at all cost,
Put their lives in danger and some lost.
When hearing the anthem, it makes them cry
A song devoted to them, their lullaby.
Some are off in faraway lands
Writing letters and praying to be home again.
They hold their own, depend on none
Knowing this is how it must be done.
So then you question the reasons why
This service member is ready to die.
On our behalf they took an oath
To defend against all, foreign and home.
These are the veterans that proudly service,
Give them the respect that they deserve

Happy Birthday Marine

Here comes another Birthday-time to reflect on the past
The journey that brought us here & friendships that last
Our brothers and sisters, and combat in arms
Let's toast to the future and hope for no harm
Let's drink a round for those not here today
For their sacrifice is the reason we have words to say
Marines are a special breed and we've proven so
In every clime in place from a few hundred years ago
What do they call us now, devil dogs, a few good men?
Elite warriors, first to fight, we're all Marines in the end
So raise your glass-what's more to say
Semper Fi Marines and Happy Birthday!

OORAH

Obsessive maybe, but not too much
Outstanding character and such
Ready to fight 'till the end
Always a little on the mend
Hell yes, this is our word
　　　OORAH Marines is what I heard!

Leaders

There are some people in this world that make a mark
Show you the reality of your dreams and the willing-
ness of your heart
They put before you goals, not so easy to attain
Make you want it more, make you struggle through the
pain
Their wisdom is our knowledge that we seek to no end
We will grow & mature and life's tests will begin
Set before us is a path that we will not travel alone
We will take another by the hand and teach them what
we were shown
And you will stand watch as we lead on
Both proud and unaware of the impact you have done

Tribe

I belong to this tribe, that you can't understand
Because I took an oath, to defend this land
I swore an allegiance, to sacrifice it all
To protect your freedoms, if they should ever fall
This life I proudly pledged, you don't see why
I could love another so much, that I could die
The brothers on my left or the sisters on my right
Are more my family now, because we've made it through the fight
They understand my words, when only my eyes speak
When a voice takes me back, and I'm all the sudden weak
They know the isolation, when peace & quiet is all I need
The instant rush I get, when others often heed
They know pain and torture, of death and despair
They recognize the voice, that always calms the fear
They know what it's like to wake-up in a cold sweat
Searching for reality, enemies' eyes met
The anxiety of being with others, the depression of being alone
The see-saw of emotions, as my anger shown
You know my intensity, because you have it too
But what do we do now, to help us get through
In this tribe, our trust runs deep
You're an outsider to us, lies is what you speak
It takes us a long time to let someone in
Because if you're not one of us, you're one of them
We're more than comrades, more than merely friends
We've each lost a part of us to become a Veteran
We may be here physically, but a change has taken place
Part of us has died, trying to keep you all safe
Please help us see
That you love us for who we are and not who we used to be
Because this is the only way you get to subscribe
Is to truly understand, that we belong to this tribe

Surmise

I imagine a world
Where I can be accepted for who I am
Where the color of my skin
Doesn't determine where I fit in
When I can sing and dance
Let my imagination run free
When you focus on the performance
The inner beauty in me
Where I'm not defined
by these narrow rules
When you realize the past
Was led by fools
To be truly exquisite
In the eyes of others
The sanctity of human life
To love one another
It's in this dream
That I conceive
To live in a world
Far better than I believe

Colonel

I laid you to rest today and I thought I had made my peace
But as I saluted your flag that I watched them fold
I realized just how little of the truth you told
I didn't know this man that others knew so well
The heroic life you led, the stories you never tell
Your bravery in service during acts of war
Medal upon medal, that I didn't know you wore
Ten years of foreign service and tours in Vietnam
30 years all together, yet you remained so calm
I wish I knew your secret or how you learned to cope
Was it grandma & your children all that gave you hope
Was it your career that kept your heart a flame
A masterful engineer refusing to be tame
Was it your love of golf, the tranquility it brings
Or playing in your garden, listening to cardinals sing
Was it your faith, the reassurance of something more
It was grandma's being, at her very core
What a love you had! More grand than I can dream
She followed you around the world, an unstoppable team
Over 60 years of marriage, four children of your own
With the passing of her sister, brought a few more in tow
And each struggle was met with a resounding promise
That together you would make it, you would show us
By your example you led the way
Two more generations of Veterans have served this day
You taught us of love, honor and respect
The tug of war of emotions when needs are not met
I learned about money and I learned about debt
I learned about hard work and regret
And this last lesson will remain forever
That life is too short for those we remember

The Graduate

Where is the man, I use to know
Not an ounce of him left to show
He's taller now, with pride in his stance
A certain resolution he's found in this chance
His conviction and trust have renewed his spirit
He anticipates the future with new merit
He's tough as nails by design
Yet remarkably honest and very kind
This process was hard, as most healing is
So much to gain when you choose to live
You've found your self-worth and aspiration for life
Your sense of purpose and being alive
I wasn't the reason, I merely lent an ear
I'm glad you trusted me and let down your fear
Because starting over is no easy task
It starts with us removing one of those masks
You know the two or three we hold
Not to let you in, the truth be told
It's part of our defenses, we know too well
No weakness shown, retreat into my shell
That was who you use to be
That's not the man in front of me
This one's courageous and he stood the fight
He's forever changed, limitless potential in sight

Clients

Can I inspire you, she wonders tonight
Is there courage within you to stand the fight
Can you be vulnerable and let me in
To discuss the unimaginable pain that lives within
Can you share your thoughts and heed my words
Find your inner peace and set aside your sword
Can you try to be present and listen at best
To these words of validation and how this is a test
Can you let me in and open the box
Let the memories flow and remove the lock
Can you still be in control and allow yourself to heal
To conquer the fear that lives within, this partnership
we seal

Setse

This isolation is comes in waves
Welcome back to the home of the brave
Where so many we lost & few are saved
And to fit in, is all we crave

Be honest & true, I know you dare
This oath we took, was more to care
Lay your burdens, it's mine to share
You're immensely brave beyond compare

You must know how we feel
Taking those drugs just to deal
Nothing more than time to steal
Here's the bullet, time to kill

Try to relate if you can
A mere ghost, instead of man
Shattered to pieces within the sand
Guess it's your turn to take a stand

So choose your weapon, face the fight
Turn from love, none in sight
Because courage will glow within this night
Pushing you forward with all your might

Beautifully Broken

They tell me to fix things and bring me the broken
But I can't change you, no truer words spoken
I can lead the way and hope you follow close
But the reality is, you do the most
I offer suggestions and we problem solve
Find the solution together, for the pain to dissolve
I teach you to listen, communication is more than
words
Body language, hand gestures, often too disturbed
How to be nice, how to do more
Not to use anger to settle the score
Expressing emotions in effective ways
That trauma you carry, begin to lay
There's more than one way to process this pain
Independently different yet identically the same
Write me a poem, paint me a picture
Tell me your sorrows, I'll be your sister
You're my brother in arms, we are a kindred spirit
You don't have to do this alone, I declare it
I have this set of skills, you know it's true
That's why you're here right, so let me help you

Work In Progress

I'm a work in progress, that's for sure
But I think time and space is my cure
The more I get to know me, the more I fall in love
I'm a pretty spectacular human, must have been sent
from above
There's got to be a plan, some route to follow
Either in the stars above, or the waters shallow
There's more for me to do, more life for me to live
More wisdom to bestow, way more gifts to give
I'm a believer in the impossible, chasing unimaginable
dreams
With a conqueror's spirit, the advisory on teams
I'm a delicate flower, in the garden I have but one spot
Yet cross me once and the wrath of hell you caught
I'm not that timid girl I was before
That ship exploded, wreckage cast about the shore
What's been rebuilt will withstand the mighty fight
I've laid these bricks myself, they shall not dawn the
light
This work in progress is not a wall around my heart
But a door instead and I choose who gets to take part

The Giver

We would give it all away if we could
We would sacrifice it all for the better good
Does that make us crazy or ambitious
Lofty and full of dreams or righteous
We see the hope within their eyes so bright
The pain ever lingering, blindly in sight
Do we give in order to receive
Is a stress free life too hard to conceive
Do these givers ever feel rewarded in the end
Do they serve so their heart will mend
Is general kindness and love for all mankind
Any part of this world in our life time
Maybe it is for those who give
Maybe they sacrifice so others can live
Isn't that the plan for us all
To leave this place better, when we get the call
To devote your life unselfishly to another
For a giver this is their life, there is no other.

Silence

I'm not sure if silence is a place or thing
A sanctity of peace or muted suffering
Do we crave the hush, the nightly gratitude
Because the chaos of the world is a new magnitude
I want the tranquility at the end of my shift
My expression of words, I shall not lift
There's something amazing when silence is heard
When you're alone with your thoughts, so undisturbed
To sink into the quiet uncomplicated resolve
Where noiseless lives and tension dissolves
This is when I find my strength
Turning off my brain, muting my think
Silence to me means all the above
Simply complicated yet masterfully loved

The Same

We walk among heroes and no one even knows.
They carry on with their lives like normal people.
They take their kids to school, buy groceries, and pay
their bills on time.
But they are different.
They enter rooms last to survey the entire space.
They sit with their back against a wall, yet facing the
entrance.
They know when a person does not "belong" in a cer-
tain place.
They notice when a car is a little too close or if none
are in sight.
Their home is checked and secured every night.
They repeat these steps every day in every situation,
yet it goes unnoticed to most people.
You call it OCD.
They call it hypervigilance.
You call it anxiety.
They call it being actively aware.
You call it anger.
They call it intensity.
You call it violence.
They call it survival.
These qualities we want in our warriors, our soldiers,
& Marines.
Yet we despise them in our husbands, wives, lovers &
friends.
The same way we embrace the veteran when they
come home and thank them for their services,
Is now the person you alienate for not being the
same?
What is "the same" after you have gone to war?
They put their life on the line to protect the freedom
of others.

They have lost friends, watched people die.
The ones they left at home are not the same either.
Those at home have delivered babies, celebrated anniversaries, and birthdays alone.
Everyone is alone.
That family back home is all the service member thought about while they were gone.
They kept him alive and now they can't connect with those people any more.
They can't talk about the horrible things they have seen.
They do not want to cause any more pain,
So they push every one way and they do what they know best.
They protect. They stand watch; they never let their guard down.
This is their blessing and their curse. They proudly accept this fate.
Not all wounds are visible, but they are just as real and painful for all involved.
These heroes among us have survived several wars,
Yet the battle of coming home is more likely to kill them.
It's our turn to be patient,
To stand watch over our warrior and to protect them from their enemies.
We have to embrace who they are today, not dwell on who they used to be.
Things will not ever be as they were before, because we have all changed.
It is our job however to embrace this change, value each day,
And honor those who have given their all so that you can still have the right to enjoy your freedoms.

 **hapter Five**

Stories– are undying and meant to be
shared. Poetry can be short and sweet,
but sometimes a story must be told;
the author weaves a plot to unfold;
and a lesson shall be taught to behold.

When we believe in the impossible, it
becomes possible, and we can do all
kinds of extraordinary things.

-Madeleine L'Engle

My Sword of Light

Just beyond the horizon, where the ground disappears
I see a reflection, it glistens between the tears
I walk faster, I run in full sprint
As I get closer, it forsakes my descent
Is it really there, what I'm searching for
Something to give me strength, to keep fighting this war
Hopeless isolation, endless thoughts of self-doubt
Needless wondering, leaves me broken throughout
I yearn to believe, in this thing called More
But as I start this journey, I'm raw to the core
I need strength, I'm ravaged by pain
Depression, anxiety, pretty much the same
I see the light, it's within my grasp
I reach for it and hope it lasts
It's heavy in my hands, yet fits my palm
It washes over me, a sudden wave of calm
My sword of light, I've found it at last
I can conquer the world, put to rest the past
Its brightness is blinding, the meaning is known
I can take my life back now, my hope is finally shown

Advocate

Advocate for support and encourage through hope
Defend against violence and teach how to cope
Valued, yet normally working behind the scenes
Overcoming obstacles to inspire dreams
Courageous and calm, they weather the storm
Ambitious and kind, their heart always warm
Time does not matter, their clock never ends
Empowering their clients until their happy ending begins

Social Worker

Social Worker, is that you
Outstanding ethics through & through
Courage to fight by all means
Integrity busting at the seams
Alliances with all mankind
Loyal and devoted 'til the end of time
Witness to all that can stand the fight
Optimistic views clearly in sight
Remarkable strength & true passion
Knowledge is our power, no better fashion
Energize the world to bring hope
Ready, is our life to devote!

Angels

Do you believe in angels, she says to herself
As she walks in and throws her keys on the shelf.
In this world where misfortune is an all too common thing,
So many times she questioned, just who is the higher being.
As she drove home from her night shift, like every night before.
She came across a stranger, coming out her building door.
Her eyes told a story, her mouth did not speak,
She slipped out of her way without a blink.
As she reached to turn the knob, she glanced behind her back.
The woman was gone, like she vanished in the black.
Just before she reached the third door on the right,
She heard a baby cry in the stillness of the night.
The cries were close, only a step or two away.
She saw a mother weeping, holding her baby is dismay.
She said she had awakened, by not hearing a sound.
Her baby not breathing is what she found.
In a fury of uncertainty, she cried out for help.
She swung open the door and found a woman there knelt.
The woman took the baby in her arms; put her mouth to his,
Blew in one great breath , and he began again.
The mother was still shaken and very distraught.
She waited until the paramedics came and took them both off.
As she walked back to her door, a single thought was on her mind.
Heaven must have sent angel to watch over us tonight.

Glass Ceilings

There are no limits to the things I can do
I'm well educated, got a few degrees too
But I'm missing this oh so important thing
This appendage I don't have is my suffering
I read and research and study it all
I've fought for so long that I can barely crawl
I've heard it all time & time again
You can't do this or that, it's only for men
It starts for us in school by what sports we can play
The clothes we wear the words we can say
No cursing, no violence, no contact sports
No standing out, no leveling of the court
Not too much make-up, watch what you wear
Don't set yourself apart to make people stare
Don't be a loner, but don't talk too much
Don't be loose, but don't let them touch
Don't stand out, but don't blend in
You can't be a two, but heaven forbid you're a ten
We are judged in every single little way
No wonder as women we have no say
If I choose to work and be a mom too
Then I'm judged and ridiculed right on cue
Because I can't possibly do both and exceed expecta-
tion
You want me to fail without hesitation
You need to knock me down a peg or two
Because success in me, means failure in you
There is no way I can cook and clean
Raise the kids, pay the bills, and go to work it seems
These equal rights we fought so hard to get
Have enabled opportunities for employment and yet

The scales are off balance because as we rise
The domesticated duties with us still lie
You've given us a mile, yet taken three fourths
We carry such a burden, yet stay the course
We let you tell us what we can or cannot do
Like we are born with a submissive bone, to just follow
you
We don't ask for the same pay
We do more than we should
We can carry the team
But be alone if we could
We see the world through a different view
Hopelessly optimistic, dreams never too few
Are women really so hard to understand
Surely yes, if explained by a man
I'd like to say that change is near
Maybe in a century there'll be less fear
Maybe the roles will reverse and you can live what I say
I can't imagine what it would be like for you that day
I have to constantly prove who I am
Like a series of tests, that has no end
With every new job or place that I move
Starts the banter of questions, just who are who
I work harder and faster, just to make you proud
So you can see my work ethic and know my values are
sound
But it will never be enough and we both know it's true
Because the evolution of change must begin within you

I'll see you in the AM

I hear the pain in your voice
I see the tears you try to hide
You've built this enormous wall
I'm beating down the door to get inside
I see you running towards the light
hoping to reach it just in time
Then you falter and retreat
Knowing it can't possibly be so sublime
What if it could be
What if through all the pain there came peace
What price would you pay
To make it all cease
Cease to empower, cease to provoke
Cease to just exist in this society is a joke
I can't relate to these people
I don't even want to try
You judge me based on your textbooks, and for that I
sign
I need to be more than a diagnosis you treat,
Symptoms & criteria, checklists you meet
I'm not the illness I suffer from
Nor am I the one still holding the gun
But that's how you see me-a danger to all
Better ship me off-get me medicated
Someone else's problem after all
But that's not what I need,
Hell I don't even know
But I can guarantee
That I'm not going through this alone

There's someone in my corner
Just like there's someone in yours
Why not let them jump in that foxhole,
And give them a tour
Because they would run away,
Or wouldn't understand
Well see, this gamble you've given up
And I haven't yet seen your hand
How do you know what I can take
If you never truly give
How many years has the past taken
And you're still not ready to live
I can't make you, but I can show you the way
My actions are honest, there's integrity in all I say
I don't have all the answers
And I may presume too much
But you can bet that I'll be there when it gets too rough
Because I want you to see the light
To heal from the outside in
To mourn the loss of your friends
To live life fully as they intend
If this was your second chance
A do-over if you will
Would you seize the opportunity
I guess only time will tell

Humanity

A final goodbye, like a curtain call, the final bow towards my friends who are not really my friends at all. It's all so fake. In world that prides itself on reality, yet no one knows what their true reality is. What's mine, what's yours, what's this country? I don't know because we are ruled by laws, not by love. We are ruled by deadlines and standards, instead of ambition and intuition. We don't value integrity or honor, just a bottom line. We should have been born in a different time. When love conquered all. When family was everything. When money didn't matter. When being a Veteran was a true testament to your morals and values as a human. In another time, we could have had it all. But not in this one. So, I bid you farewell, love, grace, and I hope one day we shall call each other friends again.

I wish upon many stars that your happiness is granted and love be among the horizons we have yet to see.

My Library

I have thirst for knowledge that can't be quenched
I'll read it all in no particular sequence
I love a good story, a plot with a twist
A murder mystery or a chance that is missed
You can keep the romance, Sci-Fi and horror
I want to learn something, knowledge is power
Research articles and self-help books galore
I need them all and I want more
I don't need fancy dinners, wine & roses too
Give me books because you know my passion is true
I want a library, filled from baseboards to beams
I'm going to read them all, let them play out in my
dreams
They provide me a window to both explore and escape
An imaginable journey in a tangible shape
They are not merely books you see
They are an undiscovered world for me
They open the door to possibilities and endless won-
der
Amazing adventures, calming peace for my slumber
They are stacked high in every room if you look
Because I will never go without an amazingly good
book!

Windows

I love how some times
You can see right through
And other times
It's a reflection of you
This house of windows
It protects me not
You said I was safe
That's what I thought
But just beyond
The window pane
I began to cower
And forgot my name
I can look out to see
All the dreams I have
Yet my heart aches
With one more stab
The coolness of the glass
Under my fingertips
The barrier it provides
The safety of all of this
The power of knowing
That I control it all
To take a leap of faith
Hoping I don't fall
Whose reflection do I
Hope to see
Looking through this window
Staring back at me
I hope it's that
Courageous one
That brave Marine
That got shit done

Or the counselor
That heals the broken
Spreading hope
With all words spoken
Maybe it's the mom
Who loves with all her might
To give her kids the world
Their happiness in sight
Or the friend
That can never be replaced
Always here for you
With a smile and embrace
Maybe it's the writer
Who inspires the masses
To bring about change
In this world she imagines
In her reflection
She sees them all
They each give her strength
And cushion the fall
She understands
What so many know
This perfect reflection
Is her window

Letter to My Younger Self

To my younger me. ....I love you. I wish this didn't happen to you. You are made for great things and one day all this crap you feel will help others. I know that's hard to imagine right now, but it will. You are going to grow up and experience real love, true, amazing, love. And you will never want it to end. But this love won't come from a man; it will come from your children. You will inspire them to follow their dreams; you will give them everything they ever wanted. But most importantly you will get to be a kid with them because you didn't have a childhood. You will have sleep overs, ice cream parties, movie nights, pajama days, and bowls of cereal for dinner. You will share your favorite books with them and they will pick up on your love for literature. You will sing out of tune. Dance for no good reason while cooking dinner. And scream "I love you" as you drop them off at school and drive away, embarrassing them by all means. You will take every opportunity to tell them just how proud you are of them and how much you love them. You will be there with answers about boys, girls, and drama. You will attend every game, performance and parent meeting for them. You will be an amazing mother because you will give them all the love you were never given. You will live your life through them; their joy will be your joy. And you will begin to pick up the pieces of your shattered past, because with every new great memory a little of that pain will go away. You are destined to change the world. Now go do it.

Defining Love

I think love is grand, ongoing and ever changing. Love to me is about how you feel, the emotional connection as well as the actions you give in return. I also think there are different kinds of love. My motherly love is not the same as the love I have for my best friend and neither of those loves are the same as the love for my partner. I think I reserve my truest form of love for my partner because he sees the raw, broken, beautiful parts of me that I keep hidden from the world. I think that is what love is about…being able to be your honest transparent self with another without the fear of judgment or ridicule, just acceptance.

I also feel that love is like a growing organism within you and with others, because it can grow stronger or weaker. I want a love that grows and grows. And I think to help it grow, you must feed it healthy doses of joy, pain, compromise, and knowledge. Love requires a constant "falling" aspect, accomplished through experiences, sharing holidays, quality time, making memories, and living life fully together. I think this is how true love works-it's not easy, it's not perfect, but it's a promise to each other to keep trying to fight for one another no matter what. That's how to keep the love alive, the organism in constant growth, because when you ignore something, it tends to die. By showing it that you don't have time, space, or needs that can be met with the other-they learn how unimportant they are in your life. That's not love, that's companionship. I want love, in its truest, deepest, magical form. How about you?

Fear

Are we scared because we think we know?
Or are we scared because we don't want to know?
Is it worth losing it all to gain something you've never experienced before?
Do you stop it now because the pain would be less than when you go on?
Or is that to say that getting your heart broken upfront doesn't hurt as bad as in the end?
Are hopes and dreams something you just wish for?
Do wishes come true?
I believe in it all...everything happens for a reason.

Dead

I'm drowning, being pulled down by a rip tide, suc-
cumbing to the water that fills my lungs as my screams
silence in the murky waters of the ocean's depths.

I'm buried alive, placed in a box, nailed up tight, with
only the tingling of the dirt touching my face to re-
mind me that I'm still alive as I'm placed in my shal-
low grave.

I'm on fire, my body blisters in the heat as my skin
responds to the flames of eternal hell without even the
moisture of a last breath to ease my suffering.

I'm shot, I feel the bullet enter me as my insides are
torn apart in mere seconds, my blood pooling around
me like a crimson dress for my final curtain call.

I'm dead. Finally my pain is gone and their healing can
begin. No more emotions to wade, no more memories
to escape, no more trauma to relive, no more disap-
pointment to see on your face. No more living be-
cause in death I cede control. This is the only way to
free my soul from the bondage of this life.

Dear John

Dear John, here's the letter I should have written long
ago
But I didn't have the courage then to let my pain show
I wanted to believe that I could give you more
That I could reach your expectations and settle the score
But I failed on a daily basis to be the wife you needed
I succumbed to your control, all power ceded
A mother, a maid, the chef, just to name a few
But a worthless person is all you viewed
I lost so many jobs and friends along the way
Starting over and over, every time you say
I blended into the background, so you could shine bright
I made every tour successful, so you could have the
limelight
I wiped away tears and raised our children alone
I took the brunt of their anger, so to you it never
showed
I begged for intimacy, acceptance, and love
I received anger and rejection, constant push & shove
I wonder now if you ever truly loved me
Based on lust, doomed to fail, you see
How well do you know this wife of fifteen years
What is my purpose in life or do you even care
How much poetry do I have, how many clients do I see
How do your bills get paid, what's a normal work week
for me
What's my fast food order, how do I take my tea
Why do I read so much, but let's not focus on only me
Tell me Julian's favorite teacher or his best friends' name
What's his favorite tv show or first pick video game

How does he like his sandwich, what's his go to snack
What does he collect, tell me one interesting fact
How about Felicity, what does she do in her free time
What's her favorite subject; in what areas does she shine
How many sports did she play this year
Who's the teacher she hates beyond compare
They seem easy enough for me, because I know them all
But you parent with financial gifts and the occasional
phone call
We all deserve to be valued and fully understood
As I break up this marriage, I know it's for the good
It's going to take time to heal and I've done my damage
too
Destroying you was not my plan, neither was starting anew
But what I need is closure and this river of tears to end
We can't be husband and wife, but we can be parental
friends
I want you to choose to be in their lives, pick them for a
change
Show them that you love them, more important every day
You must win them back, because they're ready to run
Give them a reason to believe in you that this battle
they've won
There's so much more I want to say, although you'll never
hear
It's ok, it's about me now and the closure I need my dear

The Listeners of the World

Clinicians

It takes bravery to do what we do every day. To sink our teeth into the depths of someone's worst nightmare and think we can help. We carry their traumas with us and we are forever changed with each story we hear. Their burdens become ours and we weather the storm together. We listen, we guide, and we plant seeds of hope in the most desolate areas of those that need it most. We ignite the flame to love again and provide a sounding board for reason. Courage allowed them to survive a thousand deaths and brought them through our door. It's our turn to be courageous, to stand watch over the fallen and provide them with a blanket of safety. So, they can heal, grow, and find a renewed sense of purpose in life.

The Listeners of the World

Peer Support Navigators

They are the truest form of navigation in every sense
of the word. They navigate trauma stories with endless
arrays of obstacles they must endure in order to guide
their peers back home safely. They are the ones that
can bring our fallen home, because they understand
the fall themselves. They know the depth of the hole
they have dug and they know the way out of the dark-
ness.

The Listeners of the World

Military Families

The spouses and children of military families face an array of difficulties that many people do not truly understand. What if we asked you to allow your spouse to leave for several months and told you there was a good chance they may not return or return injured? Could you maintain your job, the monthly expenses, single parenthood, all while praying for their safe return? What if we asked you to pack your belongings, leave your family and friends and move to a place you have never been? Could you find a new job, enroll your children in the new schools, find a place to live and navigate a new city? And then I reminded you that you will need to do all of those same things again in a couple of years? What if I said these children gain insight through experiences of different cultures, values, and geography? What if I said they mature faster, value family above all else, respect authority and make friends easily? These what ifs are the stories of our military families and it is our privilege to honor their sacrifice and finally allow them to be 'welcomed home.'

The Listeners of the World

A Veterans Network

Vulnerability is our specialty. We have the privilege to hear their stories, inspire them, create hope, and guide them through this powerful healing journey. We all know the saying 'it takes a village to raise a child.' It also takes a village to bring our Veterans home. They need therapists, peer specialists, integrative medicine, a true total immersion of holistic healing to begin to live again. We can provide those tools and be the first to implore our fellow Veterans to not only live, but instead to be alive. To find their value in life, their sense of purpose and renewed hope. To honor their sacrifice and most importantly to ask them, what's next. Because this is only a chapter in their story and we can't wait to hear what comes next!

Happily Divorced

It's funny when you tell people you're going through a divorce, their reaction is to say, "I'm sorry."
I don't think I understood that until today and that's where I'll begin this story.

As I packed the boxes, separated our things
I reminisced on the good times, few they seem
There's so many pictures, more albums than I can count
Such amazing memories, how to divide this families amount
I've cried more tears than I think I should
But I didn't expect this pain, it's supposed to be good
It's supposed to bring closure, a chance to be on my own
The opportunity for possibilities, a brighter future shown
But right now, I can't see past
These fifteen years and why it didn't last
Did we grow apart, did we change too much
Did we fail each other and lose touch
I know I did, I stopped believing long ago
I gave up on potential and I let this damage grow
Slowly you built this wall around my heart
Each act of malice, a new brick in part
I tried to tell you, over and over again
But you refuse to listen, not even to your friend
I walk through this house and wonder what went wrong
We point the finger at each other, new dance, same song
I admit my faults and my mistakes stack high
You won't take any of the blame, you're not that guy
So I'll carry this burden with the A upon my chest
And I'll keep reminding myself that I gave it my best
I bent so much for you that I often feel broken
Only to see it was just a game and I was without token
Of course, in hindsight we see the error of our ways
Love can make us blind, so easy to dismay

We did it all wrong, this relationship built on lust
Two lonely people in a marriage without trust
Trying to start over, running from one mess
Never dealing with our past and bringing it into this
Were we doomed to fail because we began
Knowing how it ends, would we do it again
I think the best I can do is be true to myself
Never walk in another's shadow, be a trophy on shelf
I've grown as a person, not to be who I was before
Because a transformation took place for this I am sure
Because without it, I wouldn't have the courage to leave
I'd placate your demands, tranquilize my feelings with ease
And I was good at this, I fooled myself for so long
Then something shattered in me and I knew I had it all
wrong
I forgave myself for the past that haunts my nights
I gave that little girl a voice as she trembled in fright
And as I let go of these burdens that weighed me down
That small voice inside of me begging to be happy, be-
came a roaring sound
Someone had turned on the lights, as if I lived in a cave
Showing me that after 37 years, I didn't have to be brave
That truly being seen has nothing to do with your eyes
It's the vulnerability in my heart and mind that is no long-
er disguised
I get to be myself, focus on me for a change
Discover what's been missing and what remained the same
I guess this is where the story ends
Conclusion written, time to send
We can't change the past and would we even dare
Because ultimately life is a series of tests that bring us here
And right here is exactly where I need to be
To mourn my loss, grieve the pain, and start to live beauti-
fully

Eulogy

All I want is to die a good death
To live to the fullest until my last breath
To really enjoy the time I own
To live in the moment, a new path shown
I want to be selective in the company I keep
I want to travel the world, adventure to seek
I'm tired of playing along with all the rest
Time to standout, put this knowledge to the test
To truly live, we must be vulnerable
Step out of the box and be uncomfortable
I can honestly say, that's how I live my days
I'm a gardener of hope, procuring dreams along the way
I want them to say when I die
Here lies a woman who chose to defy
To defy the odds, break away from the pack
Choosing the hardest road and never looking back
Saving the world, one Veteran at a time
Was indeed her favorite signature line
I want to truly touch all the lives within my grasp
To be a healing voice, a profound listener at last
To know what to say, when there are no words
To spearhead the revolt, with only my sword
Because sometimes words alone are not enough
You have to advocate for others, even when it's rough
You have to stand resolute, no ethics on the line
Because morals & integrity not always embody this mankind
I want them to see me for who I really am
A sister, a mother, and unbelievable friend
I hope I can teach all that I have learned
And each day lived is a brand new turn
When I wake up refreshed and alive
It's an amazing new day for me to thrive
I won't squander my time, too much to do
I need to ensure I say I love you
Because each day we live is one closer to death
So I'm going to live mine without regret

Ely

What's in a name? Is what makes it legendary who it
becomes, the path it takes or is it the giver who decides
the worthiness?

I choose to believe the former
I've been built for greatness
My eyes have seen torture
Yet shine bright with hope for those I see
My hands have worked hard day in and day out
And their embrace offers a simple understanding to
those within reach
For this age, my back has carried more burdens
Then should ever have ever been allowed
These legs have run for fear and for fun
They help me stand tall against evil and role model
strength
My heart's been broken more than once
Yet the love of others has sewn those pieces together
into a beautiful tapestry of resolve
The most amazing part of who I am is my mind
It was my refuge as a child
An escape from the chaos into a world of books filled
with knowledge, power, and imagination
I can read and retain, hear and listen
Lead others, offer hope, empathize
Because I'm so much more than the name given to me
I've created this Ely and she is remarkable

About the Author

Misty Pearl Ely, LCSW was born in Pasadena Texas and now resides in Arlington Texas with her children. She is the Clinical Director for a rehabilitation program for justice involved veterans in McKinney.

Upon graduating high school in 1997 she joined the Marines where she served on active duty for nine years as an administrative clerk. While in the Marines she married another active duty service member and traveled the world with their two children. Two Marines battling with post-traumatic stress disorder and endless anxiety could last only so long. After fifteen years of marriage they called it quits and finally sought the help they both needed. They have finally learned to love themselves and to be accepting of each others flaws.

While on active duty Misty obtained her Bachelors degree in Social Psychology. She went on to pursue a Masters in Behavioral Medicine because she wanted a better understanding of the world of pharmaceuticals and the impact on veterans. For six years after leaving the Marines, Misty worked several different positions including probation, administration at a federal prison, and substance use prevention and education. Every job she tried seemed meaningless compared to her time in the Marines; she had lost her sense of purpose. While stationed in Iwakuni Japan, Misty began working on the base with Marines and Sailors that had gotten in trouble with alcohol and were sent to her for classes. This was when she realized that working with veterans was her calling. She understood what they were going through and they understood her. The rapport was almost instant and she could feel the growing need to do more.

After leaving Japan, Misty decided to go back to school and received her Masters in Social Work, with an emphasis on military social work. She graduated in 2014 and has been a therapist to veterans in her local community ever since. Misty is currently pursuing her doctorate in education in Community Counseling: Traumatology. She has finished all of her academic classes and is working on her dissertation proposal.

When Misty is not counseling, doing homework, running her children to extracurricular activities or other mommy chores, she enjoys reading, writing, painting, and walking. She absolutely loves to teach and attends conference throughout the state to speak on veteran mental health concerns and growing needs.

"Saving the world one veteran at a time" is how she would like to be remembered. She simply wants to make the world a better place for veterans entrusted to her care and all those she calls friends.

One sentence about who she is:
She loved with every ounce of who she was, gave more than she ever had, and reminded the world that dreams do come true for those who believe in their own power, strength, and courage.